GREAT
PICK-UP
LINES

GREAT PICK-UP LINES

ISBN: 1 84161 193 X

Copyright © 2003 Axiom Publishers

All rights reserved

This book is sold subject to the condition that it shall not, by way of trade or otherwise, be lent, resold, hired out or otherwise circulated without the publisher's prior consent in any form of binding or cover other than that in which it is published and without a similar condition including this condition being imposed on the subsequent purchaser.

This edition first published by Ravette Publishing Ltd in 2003.

Printed and bound in Malaysia
for Ravette Publishing Limited,
Unit 3 Tristar Centre, Star Road, Partridge Green,
West Sussex RH13 8RA
United Kingdom

GREAT PICK-UP LINES

GREAT
PICK-UP
LINES

by Stephanie Gallehawk

ℛ
RAVETTE PUBLISHING

GREAT PICK-UP LINES

CONTENTS

History of Dating/Pick Up Lines..........7

Categories of Pick Up Lines..........11

Slap..........13

Cheesy/Romantic..........29

Straight to the Point (No beating around the bush)..........65

Confident/Arrogant..........83

Honesty (Not always the best policy)..........113

Comeback Lines..........119

Telephone Numbers..........140

Notes..........143

GREAT PICK-UP LINES

HISTORY OF DATING/PICK UP LINES

Dating/Pick up Lines from 1800 – 1830

"Good evening, I saw you at church this morning with your parents and I was wondering if you would like to go on a tandem bike ride together along the apple blossom trail."

Young people spent nearly a decade choosing a marriage partner. They were not strangers, but grew up together in unchaperoned interaction. Sexual passion was to be contained.

Dating/Pick up Lines from 1830 – 1880

"Hello, I have just taken over my Father's business where I am going to be set up financially for the rest of my life and I was wondering if you would be so kind as to allow me to call on you."

A man's readiness for marriage was seen by his ability to provide a home for his new wife.

GREAT PICK-UP LINES

Dating/ Pick up Lines from 1880 – 1920

"Hello, after speaking to your Mother, I was wondering if you would think about going for a romantic picnic in the park?"

Going somewhere became the activity of courtship by 1900. Before that, they mostly stayed at home. Sexual expression in courtship began to increase at this time.

Dating/Pick up Lines from 1920 – 1945

"Hi, I would be the luckiest man alive if you would come to the dance at the town hall with me this Saturday night. There is a party afterwards where Johnny's parents are away. Should be spiffing."

Dancing allowed a young couple the excitement of physical closeness without the dangers of sex. It was noted that "petting parties" became common in the high schools of the 1920's. Men were presumed to want sex, women were expected to control this and say no. Premarital intercourse was on the rise. Virginity, while still desirable in a bride, was no longer a requirement.

Dating/Pick up Lines from 1945 – 1960

"Hi, mind if I swing by your house later tonight in my car and take you to the lookout?"

More earnest dating would occur in high school, and "going steady" became popular. Parental reaction to going steady was not positive, especially as parents feared additional sexual experimentation.

Dating/Pick up Lines from 1960 – 1980

"Your name reminds me of a river I used to live near. Do you wanna go to this shagadelic party, baby, where we can make love with each other and maybe other people as well?"

Increased liberal view of sexuality and sexual behaviour. The age of this sexual experience also changed. In the 1970's the sexual experience occurred while going steady.

GREAT PICK-UP LINES

Dating/Pick up Lines from 1980 – 2000

"Wanna get down and dirty back at my place where I can play my new Duran Duran album? I have a new twin-share headphone set with a thumpin' sub whoofer system."

Greater opportunity for informal opposite sex interaction and dating became less formal. Listening to bad vinyl records, surprisingly, worked in luring the prey to bed.

Dating/Pick up Lines from 2000 – Future

"You might as well f**k me, because I'm going to tell everyone we did anyway."

Absolutely no tact at all. There is absolutely no hope for the future dating scene. Read on and discover.

CATEGORIES OF PICK UP LINES

1 – Slap
You just don't want to pick up.
You are quite happy in your own company.

2 – Cheesy/Romantic
These are for the experienced one line users.
A little too much thought has been placed in the process.

3 – Straight to the Point (No beating around the bush)
You have obviously no fear of rejection.
One more isn't going to matter.

4 – Confident/Arrogant
Have to get a giggle but if these do work you seriously have to doubt the mental health of you both. (pick upper and pick uppee)

5 – Honesty (Not always the best policy)
Refer to 1.

6 - Comeback Lines
Speak for themselves.

GREAT PICK-UP LINES

GREAT PICK-UP LINES

SLAP

You just don't want to pick up.
You are quite happy in your own company.

GREAT PICK-UP LINES

Excuse me, I am about to go home and masturbate and needed a name to go with the face.

Do you like to dance? Well then, could you dance so I can talk to your friend?

You're ugly but you intrigue me.

That shirt's very becoming on you.
If I were you I'd be coming too.

I need to dump my load.
Do you mind waiting for me
on the bonnet of my car?

Oh excuse me! I thought you were a moose.

GREAT PICK-UP LINES

Weren't you a woman the last time we met?

Hey Baby, as long as I have a face you'll always have a place to sit.

Do you spit or swallow?

GREAT PICK-UP LINES

Excuse me, miss,
do you give head to strangers? No.
Well, then, allow me to introduce myself.

You smell wet. Let's party.

(Look down at the crotch).
It's not going to suck itself.

GREAT PICK-UP LINES

I've had a bit to drink,
and you're beginning to look quite good.

Excuse me, was your mother bitten by an ugly dog
before you were born?

I'd really like to screw your brains out,
but it appears that someone beat me to it.

GREAT PICK-UP LINES

Baby, you're so flat you make the walls jealous.

Excuse me miss...Is your face so messed up because you fell from heaven?

Hey babe, how bout a pizza and a f**k?
(after she slaps you or leaves)
Hey! What's wrong, don't you like pizza?

Your face or mine?

I'm sorry, but have we met before? (No)
Oh, I'm sorry. I guess that it must
have been your mum.

You're a babe, right? Haven't you seen the film?

So, you're a girl huh?

Nice tits. Mind if I feel them?

Hi...Would you f**k me?
I'd f**k me, I'd f**k me real hard.

GREAT PICK-UP LINES

Can I stir your drink? Mind if I use my dick?

Hi. Are you cute?

I wanna floss with your pubic hair.

GREAT PICK-UP LINES

Fancy a f**k?

Now, Bitch!

I hate you...are you here with your friends?

GREAT PICK-UP LINES

I had sex with someone last night. Was that you?

Hey Baby...can you suck start a Harley?

Excuse me, have I f**ked you yet?

So, do you like fat guys with no money?

You are so beautiful that I would crawl ten miles
on my hands and knees through broken glass
just to jerk off in your shadow.

Yo. You'll do.

GREAT PICK-UP LINES

Nice f**king weather. Want to?

Screw me if I am wrong,
but you want to f**k me, don't you?

I bet I could guess your weight if you sat on my face.

GREAT PICK-UP LINES

What's a slut like you doing in a classy joint like this?

Hey baby...you got any diseases? Want some?

You look like a hooker I knew in Fresno.

GREAT PICK-UP LINES

You look just like my Mother.

Didn't I do your sister?

Buy me a beer, will ya hon?

GREAT PICK-UP LINES

CHEESY ROMANTIC

These are for the experienced one line users. A little too much thought has been placed in the process.

GREAT PICK-UP LINES

Can I borrow a quarter? (What for?)
I want to call my Mum and tell her I just
met the girl of my dreams.

Damn, I thought "very-fine"
only came in a bottle!

Do you believe in love at first sight,
or should I walk by again?

GREAT PICK-UP LINES

Do you have a map? I just keep getting lost in your eyes.

I know milk does a body good, but baby, how much have you been drinking?

If I could rearrange the alphabet, I'd put U and I together.

GREAT PICK-UP LINES

It's not the size of the boat.
It's the motion of the ocean.

Your Daddy must play the trumpet,
because he sure made me horny.

Is your Father a lumberjack? (No, why?)
Because whenever I look at you,
I get wood in my pants.

Oh, my sweet darling! For a moment I thought
I had died and gone to heaven.
Now I see that I am very much alive,
and heaven has been brought to me.

There must be something wrong with my eyes,
I can't take them off you.

Was your Father an alien?
Because there's nothing else like you on Earth!

You must be from Pearl Harbour,
cause Baby, you're the bomb.

Stop. Drop. And Roll baby,
cause you're on fire!

When I first saw you I almost had to
call an ambulance to take me away,
because the sight of you stopped my heart!

GREAT PICK-UP LINES

Do you have a sunburn Baby,
or are you always this hot?

Are you from Tennessee?
Cos, you're the only ten I see.

Hi, the voices in my head told me
to come and talk to you.

Are those space pants,
'cause your booty is out of this world!

If looks were against the law you'd be arrested,
booked, and jailed for life.

Who stole the stars and put them in your eyes.

(With hands on shoulders).
Oh, those are shoulder blades,
I thought they were wings.

I have only three months to live.

Are you lost ma'am?
Because heaven's a long way from here.

GREAT PICK-UP LINES

Excuse me, but I think I dropped something! MY JAW!!!

Hello, I'm a thief and I'm here to steal your heart.

How was heaven when you left it?

GREAT PICK-UP LINES

I play the field and it looks like I hit a home run with you.

If I followed you home, would you keep me?

If you were a tear in my eye,
I would not cry for fear of losing you.

GREAT PICK-UP LINES

Is there an airport nearby
or is that just my heart taking off?

What was that sound?
It was the sound of my heart breaking.

Would you touch me so that I can tell my friends
I've been touched by an angel.

GREAT PICK-UP LINES

Your legs must be tired because you've been running around through my mind all night.

Your eyes are blue like the ocean, and baby I'm lost at sea.

Your daddy must be a hunter because he sure caught a fox!

GREAT PICK-UP LINES

Baby, if you were words on a page,
you'd be what they call Fine Print!

You must be Jamaican, because Jamaican me crazy.

Do you know karate? Cause your body is really kickin'.

Your name must be Mickey because you're so fine.

You're like a dictionary, you add meaning to my life!

Hello. Cupid called. He says to tell you that he needs my heart back.

GREAT PICK-UP LINES

I must be a snowflake, 'coz I've fallen for you.

If you were a laser, you'd be set on stunning.

Damn! Somebody needs to write explosive on you, cos you're the bomb!

GREAT PICK-UP LINES

Excuse me, do you have any raisins?
How about a date?

Baby, I'm an American Express lover...
you shouldn't go home without me!

Do you know what'd look good on you? Me!

GREAT PICK-UP LINES

Do you have a mirror in your pocket,
or am I just seeing myself in your pants?

Hi, my name is milk. I'll do your body good.

Hi. Are you illegal?

GREAT PICK-UP LINES

Is your last name Gillette?
It must be because you are the best a man can get.

Do you mind if I end this sentence in a proposition?

What is your first name?
Hmm...that goes kinda well with my last name.
(switch if female asking a male).

GREAT PICK-UP LINES

Are you real? Are you really standing there?
Or is this just another dream?

Baby you must be a broom,
cause you just swept me off my feet.

Did the sun come out or did you just smile at me?

GREAT PICK-UP LINES

Have you always been this cute,
or did you have to work at it?

Hey baby you must be a light switch,
cos every time I see you, you turn me on!

I feel like Richard Gere.
I'm standing next to you, the Pretty Woman.

I hope you know CPR,
cos you take my breath away!

I just had to come talk with you.
Sweetness is my weakness.

I think I can die happy now,
'cause I've just seen a piece of heaven.

GREAT PICK-UP LINES

I'm not drunk, I'm just intoxicated by you.

Nice to meet you, I'm (your name)
and you are...gorgeous.

Was your Father a mechanic?
Then how did you get such a finely tuned body?

Were you arrested earlier?
It's gotta be illegal to look that good.

Were you in Boy Scouts?
Because you sure have tied my heart in a knot.

What's that on your face? Oh, must be beauty.
Here, let me get it off. Hey, it's not coming off!

Damn, if being sexy was a crime,
you'd be guilty as charged!

You are the only reason why I came in here alone.

If I had a rose for every time I thought of you,
I would be walking through my garden forever.

GREAT PICK-UP LINES

You are so beautiful that you
give the sun a reason to shine.

Excuse me, but does my
tongue taste funny to you?

Your ass is so nice that it is a
shame that you have to sit on it.

GREAT PICK-UP LINES

Baby, I'm no Fred Flintstone,
but I can make your Bedrock!

To a girl with braces and if you have them as well:
"Hey wanna hook up sometime?"

Hey baby...drop that zero and get with the hero,
in other words...you better come with me.

I'll be your six, if you be my nine!

I'm fighting the urge to make you
the happiest woman on Earth tonight.

As you walk by, turn around and say:
Excuse me, did you just touch my ass? No! Damn!

GREAT PICK-UP LINES

Want to see my stamp collection?

Is your daddy a thief? No!
Then who stole those diamonds
and put them in your eyes?

Bond. James Bond.

GREAT PICK-UP LINES

Stand back, I'm a doctor.
You go get an ambulance,
I'll loosen her clothes.

Love is like a rug,
so you can walk all over me
and lie on me.

Lie down. I think I love you.

GREAT PICK-UP LINES

Oh no, I'm choking!,
I need mouth to mouth quick!

Sit on my lap and we'll get things straight between us.

Excuse me, mind if I stare at you for a minute?
I want to remember your face for my dreams.

GREAT PICK-UP LINES

There must be something wrong with my eyes,
I can't take them off you.

I've seemed to have lost my number,
can I have yours?

Is there a rainbow, because you're the treasure
I've been searching for.

GREAT PICK-UP LINES

Are you cold? You should be,
you've been naked in my mind all night.

Excuse me, can you give me directions?

You are the reason people fall in love.

GREAT PICK-UP LINES

Look at the tag on the back of a girl's shirt,
when she turns around say...
"Just checking to see if you were made in heaven."

I'm Doctor Love.
Open your blouse and say "aaaaaa."

Really like your peaches, wanna shake your tree.

You know what I like about you? My arms.

I'm feeling a little off today.
Would you like to turn me on?

Hey...Didn't I see your name
in the dictionary under KABLAAM?

GREAT PICK-UP LINES

GREAT PICK-UP LINES

STRAIGHT TO THE POINT

(No beating around the bush)

You have obviously no fear of rejection.
One more isn't going to matter.

GREAT PICK-UP LINES

My magic watch tells me you are not wearing panties.
You are? It must be an hour fast!

Did you know that there are 265 bones
inside of your body? (Wait for an answer).
"Yeah, and I could show you how to get one more?"

Do you have any Irish in you?
(if no)...Would you like some?
(if yes)...Want some more?
(This works with any nationality).

GREAT PICK-UP LINES

If I told you that you had a great body,
would you hold it against me?

If I were to ask you for sex,
would your answer be the same
as the answer to this question?

I'm new in town. Could you give me
directions to your apartment?

GREAT PICK-UP LINES

Nice shoes. Wanna f**k?

The word of the day is "legs."
Let's go back to my place and spread the word.

Hi, my name is Pogo, want to jump on my stick?

Hey so you want to see some magic?
You and I will go to your place and have
sex and I'll disappear in the morning.

Have you tripped over a branch lately? (yes/no).
How about a root?

That's a nice pair of pants. Can I talk you out of them?

GREAT PICK-UP LINES

Do you sleep on your stomach?
(reply...yes/no) Can I?

Hi, I'm easy.

Are you busy tonight at 3am?

GREAT PICK-UP LINES

Stand still so I can pick you up!

Wow!!!!

Can I please be your slave tonight?

Can I see your tan lines?

Excuse me, maam, is that dress felt?
Would you like it to be?

I had a wet dream about you last night.
Would you like to make it a reality?

Here's your chance to get to know me.

I'd look good on you.

Would you please come home
with me and tie me up?

GREAT PICK-UP LINES

You know I've always wanted to sleep with you.

Hey baby...mind if I take my pants off?

I love you, you know.

Say baby, do you mind if I hangout on your
stomach for a half an hour or so?

Your father must be a farmer,
'coz you've got great melons!

Let only latex stand between our love.

GREAT PICK-UP LINES

Are you a virgin? (No). Prove it!

I don't know what you think of me,
but I hope it's X-rated.

Nice pants, can I test the zipper?

GREAT PICK-UP LINES

Is that a run in your stocking,
or is it the stairway to heaven?

So...How am I doin?

Do you have a partner? No.
Want one? (if yes) Want another one?

GREAT PICK-UP LINES

I love you. I want to marry you.
Now f**k my brains out.

Wanna f**k like bunnies?

Hey baby, let's go make some babies.

I think we must make love on the lawn
like crazed weasels...NOW!

Be unique and different, say yes.

If you want me, don't shake me,
or wake me, just take me.

Hey baby, I want to lick your thighs.

Excuse me, I've lost my virginity, can I have yours?

Pardon me, but are you a screamer or a moaner?

GREAT PICK-UP LINES

Can I flirt with you?

I bet you $20.00 you won't f**k me.

Pardon me, but what pick-up line works best with you?

Do you know how to use a whip?

Drop 'em!

Would you like to see me naked?

GREAT PICK-UP LINES

CONFIDENT ARROGANT

Have to get a giggle but if these do work you seriously have to doubt the mental health of you both.

(pick upper and pick uppee)

GREAT PICK-UP LINES

Hi, my name is...(name).
You might want to remember it now,
because you'll be screaming it later!

I've just received government funding
for a four hour expedition to find your G-spot.

Let's have breakfast tomorrow,
shall I call you or nudge you?

Wanna play midget boxing?
You get down on your knees
and give me a couple blows!

What has 148 teeth and holds back
the incredible hulk? My Zipper!!!

Would you like to dance or should
I go f**k myself again?

GREAT PICK-UP LINES

If I was a dog would you help me bury my bone?

Before you run, I am not a freak.

Come over to my house and let's do maths,
subtract the clothes, add the bed,
divide the legs and we'll multiply.

Hey...somebody farted.
Let's get out of here.

I'm good at maths. U+I=69.

Is that a keg in your pants?
'Cause I'd love to tap that ass.

GREAT PICK-UP LINES

Ever tried those prickly condoms?

Have you ever played leap frog naked?

Hey baby, let's play house,
you can be the door and I'll slam you!

GREAT PICK-UP LINES

I would say that I'm in love with you,
but you'd think I'm trying to pull a fast one.

I'm an organ donor, need anything?

I've got a pimple on my butt, wanna see it?

GREAT PICK-UP LINES

Why don't you come over here,
sit on my lap and we'll talk about
the first thing that pops up.

You have pretty eyeballs.
Of course they'd be better if they
were eyeing my pretty balls.

Hey Kitten!!! How about spending
some of your nine lives with me.

GREAT PICK-UP LINES

Have you ever played spank the brunette
...wanna try?

Hey baby there's a party in my pants
and you are invited.

Can I walk through your bushes
and climb your mountains?

GREAT PICK-UP LINES

I have a six inch tongue and
I can breathe through my ears.

Yeah, it's big and if you pat it, it spits.

How do you like your eggs in the morning?
Fertilised?

Do you live on a chicken farm? (No).
Well you sure know how to raise cocks.

Pick a number between 1 and 10.
Shit you lose now take off your clothes.

I think we might be related.
Let me check for the family birthmark
on your chest.

GREAT PICK-UP LINES

So, are you going to give me your phone number,
or am I going to have to stalk you?

Girl, if I were a fly, I'd be all over you,
because you're the shit!

Your Dad must have been retarded,
cos you are special.

GREAT PICK-UP LINES

You are so beautiful that I would marry your
brother just to get into your family.

Has anyone ever told you that you
have Scandinavian hands? (Uh...no).
No, of course not, that would be an
incredibly stupid thing to say, wouldn't it?

Can you help me find my puppy?
It went into this cheap motel.

GREAT PICK-UP LINES

Want to see my hard drive?
I promise it isn't 3.5 inches and it ain't floppy.

If you were a booger I'd pick you first.

My love for you is like diarrhoea. I can't hold it in.

GREAT PICK-UP LINES

Even though the ugly lights are shining bright,
you still look beautiful.

Hi. I'm an astronaut.
My next mission is to explore Uranus.

I have an oozy 9mm,
and I'm not talking about the gun.

GREAT PICK-UP LINES

(Approach a group of them).
I'm gonna have sex with you,
you, and you. Alright, who's first?

(Give the person a bottle of tequila).
Drink this, then call me when you're ready.

Chicks dig me. I wear coloured underwear.

(Walk over to her).
"Ok, you can stand next to me,
as long as you don't talk about it."

Sex is a killer...want to die happy?

Your name must be Daisy,
because I have an urge to plant you right now.

GREAT PICK-UP LINES

You're so hot you would roast my meat.

You know, you're very easy on the eyes...
and very hard on my erection.

I've got an itch, honey.
Lower!! Lower!! In!! Out!!

GREAT PICK-UP LINES

If I was Elvis, would you screw me?

Uh! Oh! My parents met at a place like this.
Let's get the hell out of here.

Wasn't I supposed to eat you somewhere?

GREAT PICK-UP LINES

If your right leg was Christmas
and your left leg was Easter,
would you let me spend some time
up between the holiday?

I've got a condom with your name on it.

Erections like these don't grow on trees.

GREAT PICK-UP LINES

Can you believe it?
It's been more than fifteen minutes
since I've had sex.

Hypothetically speaking,
if I were to f**k you, would you let me?

Go up to a girl, ask her:
"Do you know what winks
and screws like a tiger?"
She says no...then wink.

Have you ever kissed a rabbit between the ears?
(Pull your pockets inside out). Would you like to?

What is a nice girl like you doing
in a dirty mind like mine?

I've been noticing you not noticing me.

(Tap your thigh).
You just think this is my leg.

Hey baby, wanna
lock crotches and swap gravy?

So, howz about the two of us going back
to my place and you run your fingers
through the hair on my back?

GREAT PICK-UP LINES

Got a soggy bun for a lonely weenie?

You know, I'm not just an interesting person, I have a nice body too.

I think my medication is wearing off.

GREAT PICK-UP LINES

I'd drag my balls through a mile of broken glass,
followed by a mile of hot coals,
just to chase a laundry truck that MIGHT
have your dirty underwear on board.

Pull my finger!!!

Tickle your arse with a feather?
(What?) I said, "Particularly nasty weather."

GREAT PICK-UP LINES

F**k me if I am wrong,
but your name is Gertrude right?

I'm trying to determine after years
of therapy and lots of testing,
whether or not I'm allergic to sex.

(Wait until it gets near last call in a bar).
Find the drunkest looking woman in the place,
walk up to her, and say, "Okay, let's go home..."

I miss my teddy bear.
Would you sleep with me?

Pardon me Miss, but I can't help noticing
you have cum in your hair.

Hi, I just wanted to give you the
satisfaction of turning me down;
go ahead say no. I dare you.

GREAT PICK-UP LINES

Hi, do you speak English? (yes). Oh, me too.

You are so fine that I'd eat your poo sandwich.

Wow, your eyebrows are thick.

GREAT PICK-UP LINES

What the hell are you looking at?

You smell kinda pretty, wanna smell me?

Were you staring at my crotch?

GREAT PICK-UP LINES

GREAT PICK-UP LINES

HONESTY

(Not always the best policy)

You just don't want to pick up.
You are quite happy in your own company.

GREAT PICK-UP LINES

My zipper is reaching critical mass!

I'm collecting pubic hairs,
can I have one of yours?

So, I guess a f**k is out of the question.

GREAT PICK-UP LINES

I may not be the best looking guy here,
but I am the only one talking to you.

I just threw up!!!

Hi, my friends call me creepy.

GREAT PICK-UP LINES

I had to find out what kind of woman
would go out dressed like that.

Hi, I'm a tawdry slut looking for a good time.

Hello, I'm Mr Ed.
Want a ride?

GREAT PICK-UP LINES

You must have a nice personality.

Have you been licked
until tears roll from your eyes?

Are you free tonight or will it cost me?

GREAT PICK-UP LINES

I am very, very lonely, and I was wondering?

I'm drunk.

Like the look of your crotch.

COMEBACK LINES

Speak for themselves.

Pick up "Haven't we met before?"
Comeback "Yes, I'm the receptionist at the V.D. Clinic."

Pick up "Haven't I seen you someplace before?"
Comeback "Yes, that's why I don't go there anymore."

Pick up "Is this seat empty?"
Comeback "Yes, and this one will be too if you sit down."

GREAT PICK-UP LINES

Pick up "So, wanna go back to my place."
Comeback "Well, I don't know. Will two people fit under a rock?"

Pick up "Your place or mine?"
Comeback "Both. You go to yours and I'll go to mine."

Pick up "I'd like to call you. What's your number?"
Comeback "It's in the phone book."

Pick up "But I don't know your name."
Comeback "That's in the phone book too."

Pick up "So what do you do for a living?"
Comeback "I'm a female impersonator."

Pick up "What sign were you born under?"
Comeback "No parking."

GREAT PICK-UP LINES

Pick up "Hey Baby, what's your sign?"
Comeback "Do not enter."

Pick up "I want to give myself to you."
Comeback "I don't accept cheap gifts."

Pick up "I know how to please a woman."
Comeback "Then please leave me alone."

Pick up "If I could see you naked, I'd die happy."
Comeback "Yeah, but if I saw you naked,
I'd probably die laughing."

Pick up "Hey cutie, how bout you and I hitting the hot spots?"
Comeback "Sorry I don't date outside my species."

Pick up "Can I see you again?"
Comeback "How about never? Is never good for you?"

GREAT PICK-UP LINES

Pick Up "Hey Babe, how about it?"
Comeback "The little voices in my head are saying that it is time to take my medication."

Pick Up "I think there is something special between us."
Comeback "Any connection between your reality and mine is purely coincidental."

Pick Up "Come here often, Baby?"
Comeback "I don't know what your problem is, but I'll bet it's hard to pronounce."

Pick up "Do you want to dance?"
Comeback "What is it about no that you don't understand?"

Pick up "Would you go crazy if I went out with you for a couple of months and then left you?"
Comeback "I'd go crazy if you went out with me for a couple of months and didn't leave."

Pick up: "You and me would look sweet together on a wedding cake."
Comeback: "Only once you'd been cut in half."

Pick up "You don't sweat much for a fat lass."
Comeback "I will when I start running away from you."

Pick up "You're very attractive even though if you were any more vacuous your head would implode."
Comeback "If you were a little bit more intelligent you'd still be stupid."

Pick up: "What would you give me if I agreed to sleep with you?"
Comeback: "Syphilis."

Pick up "Nice legs. When do they open?"
Comeback "Nice mouth. When does it shut?"

Pick up "You look like you've never
done it in a water bed."
Comeback "You look like you've never done it."

Pick up "You show me yours, I'll show you mine."
Comeback "Ok, my boyfriend's over there."

Pick up "I'd like to have your children."
Comeback "Fine, they're over there."

Pick up "Can I pinch your bum?"
Comeback "Can I pinch your wallet?"

Pick up "Do you believe in sex before marriage?"
Comeback "In general, yes, but with you I'd make an exception."

Pick up "Have you ever done it with a real man?"
Comeback "No, why, have you?"

Pick up "I want to f**k you over and over again."
Comeback "I want to f**k you over."

Pick up "Are you cold, or are you smuggling tic-tacs inside your bra?"
Comeback "Are you cold or are you smuggling a tic-tac inside your underpants?"

Pick up "Can I buy you a drink?"
Comeback "I'd rather just have the money."

Pick up "Can I have your name?"
Comeback "Why, haven't you already got one?"

Pick up "What's a nice girl like you doing in a place like this?"
Comeback "Trying to avoid you."

GREAT PICK-UP LINES

Pick up "Cheer up darling, it may never happen."
Comeback "It just has."

Pick up "I never forget a face."
Comeback "Neither do I, but in your case
I'll make an exception."

Pick up "I'd like to marry you."
Comeback "I'd rather skip straight to divorce."

Pick up "I'd like to see more of you."
Comeback "There isn't any more of me."

Pick up "I'd like to take you to dinner."
Comeback "Sure, can you pick me up again afterwards?"

Pick up "I'm sure I've noticed you before."
Comeback "I'm not sure I've even noticed you yet."

GREAT PICK-UP LINES

Pick up "Kiss me and I'll tell you a secret."
Comeback "I know your secret, I work at the clinic."

Pick up "May I introduce myself?"
Comeback "Certainly, try those people over there."

Pick up "When can we be alone?"
Comeback "When we're not with each other."

GREAT PICK-UP LINES

Pick up "When should I phone you?"
Comeback "Whenever I'm not there."

Pick up "Will you come out with me on Saturday?"
Comeback "Sorry, I'm having a headache that day."

Pick up "Would you like another drink?"
Comeback "Do you really think our relationship will last that long?"

GREAT PICK-UP LINES

Pick up "Would you like to come for a drink with me next week?"
Comeback "I'm not thirsty."

Pick up "Are you happy?"
Comeback "I was."

Pick up "Bond. James Bond."
Comeback "Off. Piss off."

GREAT PICK-UP LINES

Pick up "Do you come here often?"
Comeback "Not if you do."

Pick up "Is it hot in here or is it just you?"
Comeback "It's hot."

Pick up "When I'm with you I feel like a real man."
Comeback "So do I."

GREAT PICK-UP LINES

Pick up "Why not be original and say yes?"
Comeback "No."

Pick up "You've got great boobs."
Comeback "So have you."

Pick up "I've come from another planet to seek out beautiful life forms."
Comeback "Is that because your race is so ugly?"

Pick up "Let's skip the awkward beginning and pretend that we have known each other for a while."
"So, how's your Mum?"
Comeback "She told me I wasn't to see you any more."

Pick up "You're the most beautiful looking person I've ever seen."
Comeback "So what makes you think I would want to talk to you, then?"

Pick up "What's it like being the most attractive person here?"
Comeback "You'll never know."

GREAT PICK-UP LINES

TELEPHONE NUMBERS

Name   Telephone Number

TELEPHONE NUMBERS

Name	Telephone Number

GREAT PICK-UP LINES

TELEPHONE NUMBERS

Name   Telephone Number

NOTES

NOTES